MICHAEL OWEN'S SOCCER SKILLS

MICHAEL OWEN'S SOCCER SKILLS

HOW TO BECOME THE COMPLETE FOOTBALLER

Michael Owen

with Dave Harrison

Coaching Consultant • Simon Clifford

Skills Photography • Clive Brunskill

CollinsWillow

An Imprint of HarperCollins*Publishers*

First published in 1999
by CollinsWillow
an imprint of HarperCollins*Publishers*
London

The HarperCollins website address is:
www.**fire**and**water**.com

A CIP catalogue record for this book is available from the British Library

ISBN 0 00 218935 6

Cover and text design by Rob Kelland and Adrian Waddington
Illustrations by Jimmy O'Leary and Marcus Oakley

Colour origination by Saxon Photolitho, Norwich

Printed and bound in Great Britain by Scotprint Ltd, Musselburgh

Contents

A life in football

*'We could have something special here.
If he can develop some pace, he's going
to be some player.'*

TERRY OWEN, MICHAEL'S FATHER

My first memories of playing football are of very happy times spent with my dad and older brothers Terry and Andrew. At every opportunity, we would head for the park near to our home and spend hours kicking a ball about.

They did not need too much persuading to join me. We were a football-mad family. My dad Terry had been a professional with Everton in his younger days, before moving on to play for Bradford City, Chester, Cambridge United, Rochdale and Port Vale. My brothers grew up watching him and trying to follow in his footsteps, and while he had finished playing competitively by the time I was old enough to take an interest, he loved to take his three sons for a game in the park.

They were not always tame affairs. I would usually team up with Dad and we would play two-a-side matches with jackets down for the goalposts. Even at the age of five and six,

■ *Breaking the goalscoring record for Deeside Primary School, aged 11. The first of many trophies in my career.*

I wanted to win badly and experience the thrill of scoring goals. Dad reckons I was a goal-poacher from the day I was born.

He and my mum Janette still laugh about how I used to hang around the goals, whether it was during those fun games in the park or when it got to more organised stuff with my first junior teams, waiting for the chance to slot the ball past the goalkeeper.

But he recalls there was something special about how I did it. Whereas most kids of that age would try to blast the ball as hard as they could into the net, I would try to place it accurately into the corners. I do not know whether it was because I was quite small for my age and could not generate much power but Dad reckons I had a good sense of timing and fine positional sense.

> *'If you are small and skilful and determined enough, you can stand out even more effectively'*

It was impossible to predict what sort of progress I would eventually make but Dad obviously recognised some potential and one day quietly said to Mum: 'We could have something special here. If he can develop some pace, he's going to be some player.'

I never saw my lack of height as a handicap. I was smaller than most boys of my age and when I started playing for Mold Alexander junior team and came up against opponents two and three years older, my lack of inches was even more noticeable. I got my fair share of bumps and bruises like the rest but was quick enough to stay out of too much trouble and even then had the ability to ride the strongest of tackles.

At first Dad had to persuade Mold to let me join them because I was only seven years old and their youngest side played in an Under 10s

You're never too small

I would urge youngsters never to be discouraged by the argument that they are too small. It is easy to catch the eye if you are a big kid and can belt the ball the full length of the pitch. Those are the sort of players who tend to grab more attention when they are very young. But I reckon if you are small and skilful and determined enough, you can stand out even more effectively. You start to develop in size and strength in later years, by which time some of the big lads have been found out for their lack of skills.

■ *As a youngster I was still developing my speed on the ball. But I was determined to succeed, despite the bumps and bruises.*

league. They were not too keen initially but agreed to let me go and train with them and before long I was picked for the team. I felt

Speed check

The ability to run quickly has been one of my great assets as a footballer. I suppose I was born with a certain amount of natural speed because I have never had to work on it. Since becoming a full-time professional footballer, I have kept myself sharp with sprint sessions at the training ground, but I doubt whether I would win too many races over 100 metres these days.

Over 30-50 metres, I would fancy my chances against anyone. A burst of acceleration over those kind of distances are vital to a striker when he is racing on to the ball with a defender in pursuit.

A LIFE IN FOOTBALL

10

really proud when I was given my first full kit to wear and it was not long before I began banging in the goals.

When I was eight, I started playing for the Deeside Primary Schools district side and for the next three years I scored goals so prolifically that I guess that is when I really began to make people sit up and take notice of me. I was averaging three goals a game and in one season I managed to do something which still stands as one of my proudest achievements.

I beat the scoring record previously held by the former Liverpool striker Ian Rush, who was always one of my heroes. Ian scored 72 goals in a season and I went one better in exactly the same number of games. I went on to finish that campaign with 97 and it was around that time that scouts from the professional clubs such as Liverpool, Everton, Manchester United, Wrexham and Sheffield Wednesday started to approach me.

All of them wanted me to go and train with them but there was a

strict rule laid down by the Deeside Schools FA that no player could be associated with a professional club while playing for their teams. It did not bother me too much. I knew that if I kept on improving, an opportunity would arise at a later date.

When I moved on to secondary school at Hawarden High, sport became the dominant feature of my life. I used to play for the school football, rugby and cricket teams. I was also keen on athletics and loved schools' sports days when I could show off my prowess as a sprinter. The pace which my dad was looking for when I was younger had gradually begun to develop. Unfortunately, I was still quite a bit shorter than most of the kids in my year and, unlike in football, that was a

■ *Graduation day from the FA School of Excellence at Lilleshall with, among others, Wes Brown and Michael Ball. Then it was on to Liverpool and a YTS contract.*

11

handicap when it came to sprinting. During my first two years at high school, I would find I was unbeatable at 100 metres races – but only for the first 30 or 40 metres. After that the taller lads would stretch out with their longer strides and overtake me. As I grew, I lost none of my speed, and by the time I had reached years three, four and five, I was winning most of my races.

'I felt homesick [at Lilleshall] for the first few weeks'

While I was at Hawarden High, I was invited to train with Liverpool. There was a lot of interest in me from a wide variety of clubs, but the choice was left entirely up to me. As a young lad, I grew up supporting Everton. I suppose that was because Dad used to take the family along to Goodison Park. As one of their former players, he found it easy to get tickets. Oddly enough Mum was a Liverpool fan, though it did not seem to cause problems in the Owen household!

I think I eventually chose Liverpool because I felt so comfortable there. There was a really friendly, homely atmosphere about the place and the youth development officer Steve Heighway and the rest of the staff made me exceptionally welcome, keeping me well supplied with boots, kit and match tickets.

It was on Liverpool's recommendation that I was able to take a vital leap forward with my football education. They put my name forward

■ *The tropical heat of Malaysia didn't prevent me enjoying the IXth World Youth Championships – despite the close attentions of the opposition!*

as a candidate for the Football Association's School of Excellence at Lilleshall in Shropshire and I was delighted when I was accepted in 1993. It meant moving away from home and receiving specialist training from the FA's coaching staff and receiving my full-time education at the nearby Idsall High School.

I was 14 at the time and the thought of having to leave my family was a real wrench. I felt homesick for the first few weeks, as did most of the lads. One of the youngsters a year

below me could not cope with the way of life at all and he went home. His name is Alan Smith, who has since gone on to have considerable success as a professional with Leeds United, so obviously his decision to leave the school was the right one for him.

I soldiered on and once I got to know the rest of the lads, I thoroughly enjoyed it. I believed it was the best way to advance my hopes of becoming a professional so I was willing to put up with my early homesickness.

Besides, Lilleshall was only about 45 minutes by road from where my family lived and they would often call in to see me at weekends.

While I always looked forward to their visits, I soon got used to the new lifestyle. I made some good friends among my fellow students, of whom several have gone on to make the grade as professionals such as Wes Brown, of Manchester United, Michael Ball, of Everton, Kenny Lunt, of Crewe Alexandra, and Jon Harley, of Chelsea.

We lived in hostel-type accommodation at Lilleshall and during the day went to Idsall High School, where we were treated no differently to any of the other pupils. I have to admit that my favourite activities at school came during the break-times when we could have a kickaround. There never seemed to be enough hours in the day for me to play with a football. By now I had made my mind up. I wanted to

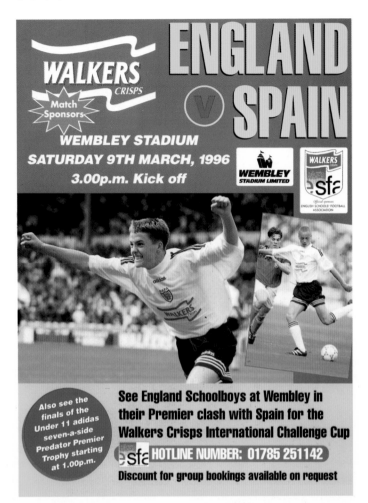

■ *No Gary Lineker in sight... the big clash between England Schoolboys and their Spanish counterparts at Wembley in March 1996.*

play the game for a living and as a consequence nothing else mattered to me.

Inevitably, my school lessons came a poor second on my list of priorities. I ended up passing all 10 of my GCSE's but most of my grades were C's and D's. If I had applied myself more thoroughly, I could have done a lot better but football had become my total obsession at this stage of my life.

I suppose that does not set a very good example to youngsters because it is vital to have

career alternatives in mind along with academic qualifications to back them up. But I was so determined to become a footballer and had already been given a fair indication by Liverpool that they were going to take me on trainee forms. As a result, my schoolwork suffered.

Once we had finished lessons each day, we would get down to the serious business of improving our football skills. We would train from 4 pm to 6 pm and after a shower and dinner, the hardest part of the day was to have to

A LIFE IN FOOTBALL

14 ■ *My goals helped Liverpool secure the Youth Cup in 1995–96.*

sit down and do our homework. It was a fairly set routine but I loved my two-year stay at Lilleshall, especially when I was selected for the England Under-16 side. It was a proud moment when I received my cap from former international Jimmy Armfield at a graduation ceremony to signal the end of the course.

Pulling on the England shirt and looking down at the three lions still sends a tingle down my spine, so you can guess what it felt like to represent my country at the various age groups. I kept up an impressive record of scoring on my debut for England at Under-15, -16, -18, -20 and -21 levels. I only played once for the Under-21s, against Greece, when I managed to get on target in a 4–2 victory. After that I was promoted straight into the full squad, where unfortunately I was unable to continue my debut scoring sequence in the 2-0 defeat by Chile at Wembley in February 1998.

After graduating from Lilleshall, I was immediately offered the chance to sign YTS forms at Anfield and I grabbed it with both hands. My apprenticeship on the Liverpool staff lasted just five months before I was given a professional contract. It was all happening so quickly I barely had time to catch my breath, but my career continued to leap forward.

I would never complain about my lifestyle.

Football has already given me the sort of things I could never have dreamed of and the occasional lack of privacy is a small price to pay for them. I have to stop and remind myself sometimes that it has all happened so quickly.

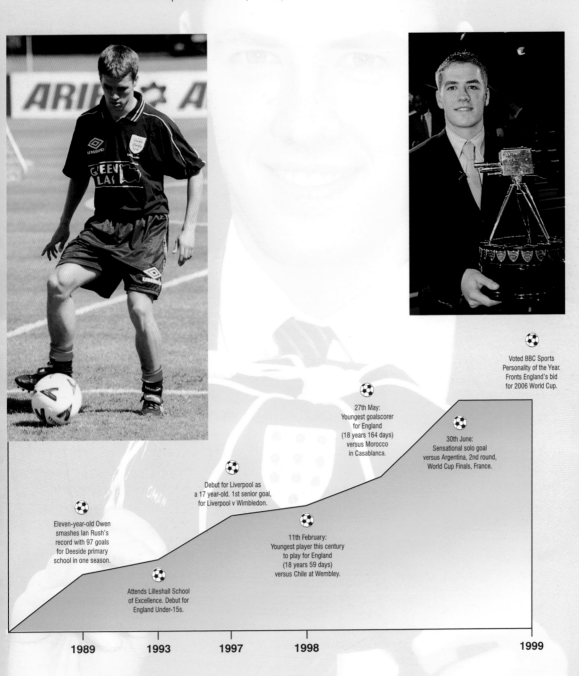

A LIFE IN FOOTBALL

15

Voted BBC Sports Personality of the Year. Fronts England's bid for 2006 World Cup.

27th May: Youngest goalscorer for England (18 years 164 days) versus Morocco in Casablanca.

30th June: Sensational solo goal versus Argentina, 2nd round, World Cup Finals, France.

Debut for Liverpool as a 17 year-old. 1st senior goal, for Liverpool v Wimbledon.

Eleven-year-old Owen smashes Ian Rush's record with 97 goals for Deeside primary school in one season.

11th February: Youngest player this century to play for England (18 years 59 days) versus Chile at Wembley.

Attends Lilleshall School of Excellence. Debut for England Under-15s.

1989   1993   1997   1998   1999

Preparation for playing

While it is tempting to rush straight out onto the pitch and start kicking a ball, it can be a foolish thing to do. It is important to get the blood flowing freely around the body and to make sure the muscles are warm before playing in a match or taking part in any work with the ball. Without proper preparations, players risk suffering torn or strained muscle injuries, so it is worth spending that extra bit of time making sure the body is ready for action.

16

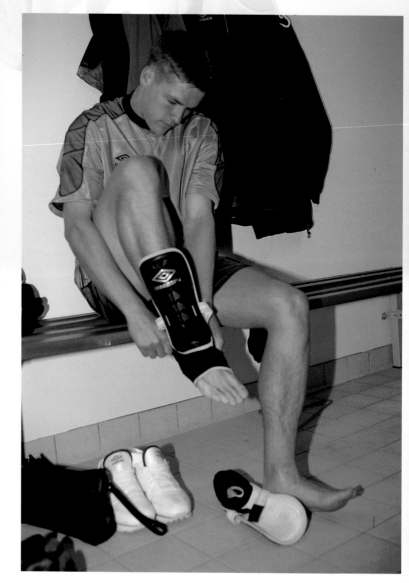

■ Be prepared before you play – having the right gear is essential for that all-important game.

■ *Loosen up the muscles by jogging the full width of the pitch and back.*

17

WARM UP

Running and stretching exercises have become necessary in all forms of football. You can start with a gentle jog across the full width of the pitch and back, varying the stride pattern by running sideways, and, at intervals, picking up your knees and lifting your heels high behind you. You can gradually pick up speed and finish with a flat out sprint across the pitch.

18

STRETCHING EXERCISES

In between each run you should do some stretching exercises. Although this is not as important for younger kids, it is a good habit to get into. The four sets of muscles you need to work on are the calf, groin, quadriceps and hamstrings. I tend to start at the bottom of the leg and work upwards.

• Calf

For the calf muscle, you should bend your front leg out ahead of you until you feel comfortable and stretch your back leg behind you, keeping it straight. Then rest both hands on your front knee and push until you feel the calf muscle stretch. With all muscle exercises, don't overdo it because that will cause the very damage you are trying to avoid. The exercise should only last about 10-15 seconds for each leg.

'With all muscle exercises, don't overdo it, because that will cause the very damage you are trying to avoid'

• Quads

Stand on one leg and make sure you are well balanced. Then grip the other foot and gently pull it up towards your backside – not too hard, just enough until you feel the muscles extend.

• Hamstrings

Stretch one leg out straight in front, digging your heel into the ground and kneel on your back leg. Grab the toe of your front leg and pull it back towards you.

• Groins

The groins can be stretched by standing with your feet apart and pointing one foot away from you with the other foot pointed straight ahead. Lean forwards and stretch your arms to the side towards the foot which is pointing away from you. Then do the same stretching to the other side, not forgetting to change the direction of your foot.

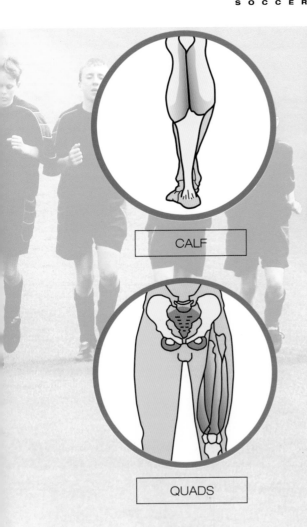

CALF

■ *Hamstring stretch.*

QUADS

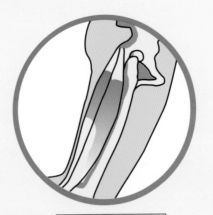

HAMSTRING

• CALF MUSCLES
help generate shooting power.

• THE QUADS
add extra running and shooting power.

• HAMSTRINGS
give you that speed off the mark.

• THE GROINS
must be strong for twisting and turning.

GROIN

Eating the right foods

A good diet has become a vital feature of a footballer's preparation. We have our own dieticians at Anfield and they are very strict about what we should and should not eat.

On match days we have to eat something which is easily digested. My choice is chicken and rice, while other players prefer baked beans or fish. It has also become popular to eat something immediately after a game nowadays. The idea is to replace the energy that has been lost during a match, especially if you have another one coming up in a few days time.

Drinking plenty of liquids before and during a game is also highly recommended. Unless you feel thirsty, you tend not to drink anything but that's the wrong way to go about it. If you wait until you are thirsty, it means you are already dehydrated and it is more difficult to replace the fluids your body has lost.

■ *A well-balanced diet requires strict discipline!*

■ *Quad stretch.*

At Liverpool, we tend to go out onto the pitch about 20-30 minutes before the kick-off for our warm-up before returning to the dressing room. Even then it is important to keep the muscles active so we carry on doing our stretches up to kick-off time rather than sit around getting cold.

20

■ *Warming-down after strenuous exercise is just as important as the warm up.*

WARM DOWN

Once a game is over, it is easy just to flop in the corner and have a rest – but it is not the right thing to do. In the same way you warmed up the muscles before a game, it is imperative to warm them down afterwards, so do your stretching exercises when you get back to the dressing room. At Liverpool we have to report to the training ground the day after each game. Even if you have not picked up an injury, the club believe it is necessary to recover properly from the previous day's activities by having a soak in a hot bath, a sauna or a massage or even a light jog.

Getting to know the ball

22

Treat the ball as a vital part of your skills development, and you will always feel comfortable on it.

All players would be lost without one – so never take the ball for granted. It should be a footballer's best friend, so you should treat it with a lot of care and attention. But before you can regard it as a pal, you have to get to know the ball really well.

You cannot achieve anything in the game without feeling relaxed on the ball and the first thing all players must do is to learn how to keep it under control, ideally with both feet, whether you are running at speed or standing still.

'Never shy away from spending as much time with the ball at your feet as possible'

IMPROVING YOUR TOUCH
There are a number of drills which are designed to improve your touch and they are good fitness routines as well. Personally, I never did many set exercises with the ball when I was younger. I learned my skills down at the park playing with my dad and brothers or kicking the ball around the back garden by myself.

You can never spend too much time with the ball when you are young. It should almost feel like it is attached to your body.

Having grown up with a ball at my feet, it became second nature to me to control it and run with it. Much of my improvement came

Michael Owen's

without me even realising it. After a while it became so instinctive, I did not even have to think about how to bring the ball under control.

But it only came after hours and hours of practice and repetition, so you should never shy away from spending as much time with the ball at your feet as possible. And if you can master the drills as set out in this book, you should be ready for anything.

Practice Drill

1 *Keep the ball within easy reach – don't stretch for it.*

2 *Use all the parts of the body, trying to keep yourself supple.*

3 *Make sure you always feel balanced – and try to keep your eyes on the ball.*

4 *See if you can catch the ball on the instep and make it feel as if it is attached to your body.*

5 *Lift the ball back into the air and use the upper parts of the body to get a good feel of it.*

GETTING TO KNOW THE BALL

23

Practice Drill

1 *Start jogging on the ball by, firstly, placing the studs of the right foot on top of it.*

2 *Remove the right foot and place the left foot on top without actually moving the ball.*

3 *Develop a smooth rhythm and change feet without stopping between touches.*

24

■ *Once you have mastered jogging on the spot, move the ball slightly in front of you as you change feet and gradually use the inside and outside of the feet as well as the soles.*

■ *It is all about control. You should be the master of the ball – not the other way around.*

skills check

- *Light on your feet*
- *Concentration*
- *Balance*
- *Composure*

STARTING SMALL

A football is always the same shape but it does come in different sizes. It does not matter how small, it is worth carrying a ball around with you to practice. When I was younger, I usually had a tennis ball in my pocket and at every opportunity I would kick it around, either with my mates in the playground or on my own up against the school wall. Then

when I moved back to playing with a bigger ball, it was amazing how much simpler it was to control it.

We have even used that kind of thing at England squad get-togethers. We would start by using a size three ball in training and you had to concentrate really hard to master control of it. Then when we reverted to a full size ball, the game suddenly seemed a whole lot easier to everyone.

Possession is everything in football. Yet the amazing thing is, the further you go in the game, the less time you spend on the ball. As a kid, I would run around with it for hours in the park and even

when I started playing junior football, I tended to hold onto it longer than anyone else to satisfy my obsession for scoring goals.

Now as a professional, I see far less of it. It is reckoned that on average, a player is only on the ball for around 60 seconds in the whole game. That makes it even more vital not to waste possession of it. The easiest way to upset your manager or team-mates is to give the ball away.

The best way to avoid doing that is to know how to receive it, control it and find a team-mate with it. Or better still, why not stick it in the back of the net!

25

Kicking, passing and moving

Now you have got a feel for the ball, the next thing to do is to learn to kick it properly. There are various ways of kicking, using different parts of the foot – with the inside, instep and outside of the boot. The first priority is to be able to kick it accurately. Power can come later.

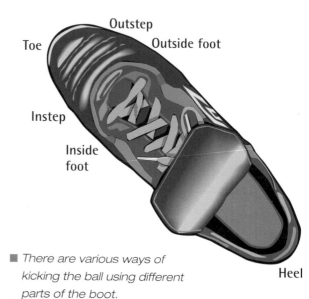

■ *There are various ways of kicking the ball using different parts of the boot.*

Outstep
Toe
Outside foot
Instep
Inside foot
Heel

26

THE SIDE-FOOT

For kicking it is best to start with the inside of the foot because that offers the widest surface to make contact with the ball and so there is less room for error. The side-foot is usually used for short, sharp passes or, if you are close enough to goal, to steer the ball wide of the goalkeeper into the net.

You should place the non-kicking foot alongside the ball pointing towards the area where you want to pass the ball, swing back the other leg and bring the inside of your foot into

> _'All the best players_
> _think one step ahead'_

firm contact with the ball with a smooth, flowing action.

Your body should be leaning slightly forward to bring your head over the ball, with your arms held out slightly to give you a better balance.

THE INSTEP

You will soon realise that you cannot generate too much power from the side-foot. For that you need to use the instep. The basic action is the same, only instead of striking the ball with the inside of the foot, swing your leg through straighter so that you make a solid contact, not forgetting to keep your body leaning slightly over the ball.

When you have mastered those two, you can really start to get clever and learn how to chip and swerve the ball. The ability to pass the ball either around or over the top of an opponent is an important part of a footballer's bag of tricks and can be easily achieved with a reasonable amount of practice.

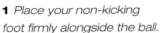
Practice Drill

1 _Place your non-kicking foot firmly alongside the ball._

2 _Lean the body over the ball as you make contact._

3 _Strike the ball solidly with the hard part of your instep._

4 _A long, smooth follow-through will help your power and accuracy._

Practice Drill

1 *Approach the ball straight on and keep your body and head leaning well forward.*

2 *Swing your kicking leg back with a short backswing and aim underneath the ball.*

3 *Stab at the ball as near to the bottom as possible with a good clean contact.*

THE CHIP

There are a couple of ways of chipping the ball. For both you should place your non-kicking foot alongside the ball and bend the knee slightly. Then with your kicking foot, you should stab at the ball as near to the bottom of it as possible with virtually no follow-through and this will lift it off the ground.

The second method is slightly more difficult. The basics are the same but this time you

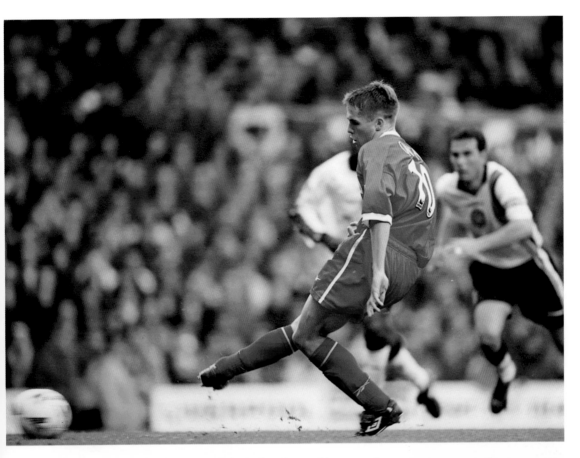

should stab down more on top of the ball and use a bit more of a follow-through. This enables you to put some backspin on it and is a very useful passing technique because it makes it easier for the receiver to control the ball. You see David Beckham use this skill a great deal.

PUTTING SWERVE ON THE BALL

The Manchester United and England player is also a master at swerving the ball around opponents, using both the inside and outside of the foot. At first, you will find it is very much a case of trial and error to see how much 'bend' you can get on it.

Starting with the inside of the foot, you should point you non-striking foot about 15–20 yards away from the target you want to reach. If you are kicking with your right foot, you should strike the ball on its right hand side about halfway up, using the area of your foot just below the big toe. You should use a long follow-through once you have made contact with the ball. It will

Practice Drill

1 *Fix your eyes on the side of the ball as you approach it.*

2 *Place the non-striking foot 18–20 inches away from the ball at an angle.*

3 *Cut across the ball and make contact with the toes on the outside of the striking foot.*

4 *For greater power, strike it lower down on the rim of the sole of the boot.*

take a while before you can swerve the ball to your intended target but keep practising.

To swerve the ball with the outside of your foot you need to place your non-striking foot further away from the ball to allow you to swing your other foot across the side of the ball. You should make contact with your toes on the upper part of the boot, again making sure to use a long follow-through. If you want to hit the

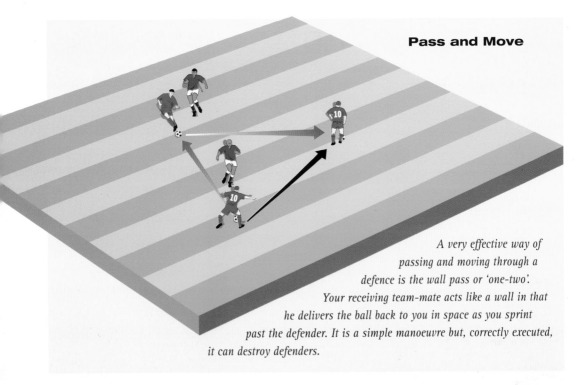

Pass and Move

A very effective way of passing and moving through a defence is the wall pass or 'one-two'. Your receiving team-mate acts like a wall in that he delivers the ball back to you in space as you sprint past the defender. It is a simple manoeuvre but, correctly executed, it can destroy defenders.

ball with greater power, you can strike it lower down on the rim of the sole of the boot. This is a method used by Brazilians like Roberto Carlos and, while you might lose a bit of accuracy, it doesn't half fly and swerve through the air if you connect properly.

PASSING AND MOVING

Being able to pass the ball is fine but once you have mastered the art and found your colleague with a perfectly-weighted pass, it is no good just standing back and admiring your work. You should always be on the move and constantly interchanging positions with your team-mates so as not to allow your marker to keep you out of the game.

All the best players think one step ahead. Even before you have received the ball, you should have some idea of what you are going to do with it. As a striker I have to be ready to lay it off quickly to a team-mate and turn into

skills check

- *Good technique*
- *Eyes on ball*
- *Think ahead*

31

space to receive a quick return. If you can do this swiftly you will always keep the defenders in a spin.

Shooting for goal

Shooting for goal

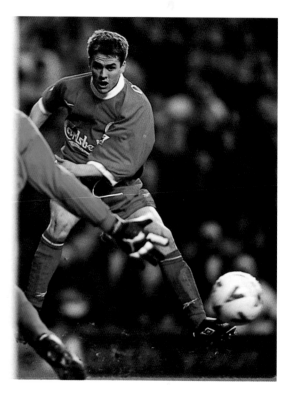

'I have always enjoyed the thrill of burying the ball past the goalkeeper'

■ *It is always a battle of wits with the goal-keeper as to who makes the first move.*

34

There is an old saying in football that if you don't buy a lottery ticket, you'll never win a prize. It usually applies to strikers and it means if you don't shoot often enough, you will never score. It was something I never really had to be taught because for as long as I can remember, I have always enjoyed the thrill of burying the ball past the goalkeeper.

GOOD PLACEMENT

I discovered when I was a young kid that you did not have to blast the ball into the net. My dad noticed, even during our games in the park, that I had a knack for slotting the ball home. I learned at a very early age that if you place the ball accurately enough, the goalkeeper will find it much harder to save than if you belt the ball straight at him. A large percentage of my goals later in my football life have come from in and around the six yard box.

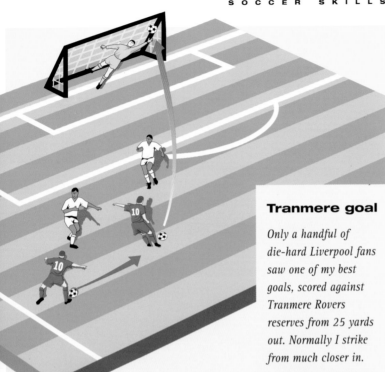

SHOOTING FROM DISTANCE

Few of my goals are scored from distance, though I surprised myself early in my Liverpool career with a goal I scored against Tranmere Rovers reserves. I cut in from the left wing and drilled the ball with my instep towards the goal from about 25 yards. It started off at a low trajectory and then took off and rose into the top corner. I did not realise I could kick the ball that hard, but my timing was just right. Dad has kept a video of that goal and still shows it occasionally just to remind everyone that it was me who scored it!

Tranmere goal

Only a handful of die-hard Liverpool fans saw one of my best goals, scored against Tranmere Rovers reserves from 25 yards out. Normally I strike from much closer in.

SHOOTING FOR GOAL

35

Practice Drill

1 *Point the non-striking foot towards the target and draw back the other foot.*

2 *Use a wide area with the inside of the foot as this gives you greater accuracy.*

3 *With a good firm contact try to steer the ball into the corner of the net.*

It is crucial to have loads of ammunition at your disposal if you want to be a prolific goalscorer. That means being able to beat the goalkeeper with a wide variety of shots, using different parts of the foot.

I have explained how I tend to use the inside of the foot when I am close to goal because accuracy is more important in these situations than power, but there are times when you need to vary your shots to try to deceive the keeper.

That is why it pays to practise the various ways of kicking the ball, because they all come in useful when you are faced with a giant of a goalkeeper who will do all he can to block your route to the goal.

■ *To bend the ball with the inside of the foot, strike it with the lower instep, just on the side of the ball. You almost have to wrap your foot around it to get it spinning through the air.*

■ *Striking the ball with the outside of the foot near the toes will make it bend the other way and you can develop more power by using the harder rim of the sole of the boot.*

36

skills check

- *Balance*
- *Technique*
- *Element of surprise*
- *Good placement*

SHOOTING FOR GOAL

37

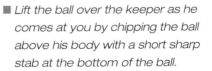

■ *Lift the ball over the keeper as he comes at you by chipping the ball above his body with a short sharp stab at the bottom of the ball.*

Dribbling

There is nothing so exciting in football than to see a player running with the ball at his feet and taking on the opposition – unless you are a defender of course. It is the thing they dislike most because they are at a real disadvantage when a forward comes at them at top

'Even before I received the ball from David Beckham, I had a clear idea of what I was going to do'

speed. They are unsure which way he will take the ball and they know that if they mistime their tackle, they will concede a free kick and possibly earn a yellow or red card.

So from an attacker's point of view, the art of dribbling is something you must learn. When you are running with the ball it is best to keep it no more than 30 to 40 cm away from your feet. You can manipulate the ball in front of you using the inside and outside of both feet and even the soles of your boots.

PROTECT THAT BALL!

Start off with a slow jog and keep your eyes on the ball. But as you progress and build up your speed, it is important to be able to lift your head so you can be aware of what is going on around you. You will need to spot a defender coming in to challenge, to notice a colleague in position to receive a pass or to try an attempt at goal yourself.

When you have gained in confidence, you will be able to pick your head up and still see the ball through the bottom of your eyes. It sounds awkward but it is possible. As you are running keep your body crouched slightly over the ball and your arms out to protect you from defenders.

Sometimes you might need to use body strength to force your way through a gap between defenders. When they are pushing and pulling at you, it is often difficult to keep on your feet let alone keep control of the ball. But if you are determined enough and have good balance, there is usually a way through.

Practice Drill

DRIBBLING

39

1 *Make sure you have good control of the ball by using the inside and outside of both feet.*

2 *Note the distance between the ball and the feet, and the eyes focused on the ball.*

3 *Balance is vital. It gives you the platform from which to change direction in an instant.*

Practice Drill

1 *You must be able to change direction while dribbling and this is a useful drill to try out. Start with the ball at your feet.*

40

2 *Dribble at medium pace between two rows of cones which should be around 5 metres apart.*

3 *As you reach the opposite cone, turn sharply using the outside of your foot against the ball, and return towards the direction you have just come.*

USING YOUR OTHER FOOT

Another good ploy if you are being pressed by a defender is to transfer the ball on to the foot which is furthest away from him. This enables you to use your body as a shield and makes it more difficult for him to get in a tackle.

The need to use both feet becomes vital during the art of dribbling. It is important to develop your weaker foot, but in my opinion you should not spend too much time on this because it will affect the development of your stronger one. That applies to shooting and controlling the ball, as well as running with it.

■ *I have lost count of the number of times I have been able to race through a defence with the ball at my feet.*

DRIBBLING

41

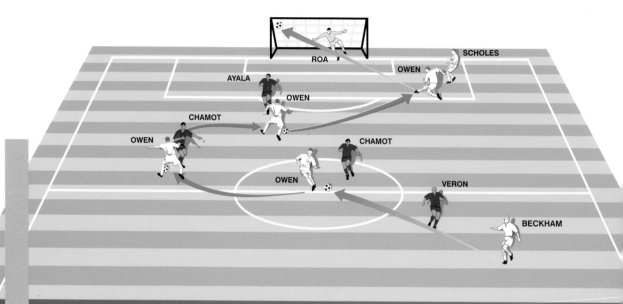

England v Argentina, World Cup 1998

When I first received David Beckham's pass there was a defender still alongside me and I had to take an early touch to enable me to get away from him. Once I had left him behind I could see just one Argentina player between me and the goal. I knew that if I could get past him I would score.

I knocked it quite a way past the last defender and used my pace to surge by him. You can afford to kick it further ahead of you if there is sufficient clear space.

Out of the corner of my eye I saw another player converging on the ball. Fortunately he was wearing a white shirt. It was Paul Scholes. For a moment I thought he was going to beat me to it and take the ball on himself. But having run that far, I was not going to give up the opportunity to score. In the end it was just me and the keeper. As he came off his line, I lifted my shot over him into the net.

However long I play football, I know I will always be remembered for the goal which changed my life. Yes, the one against Argentina in the World Cup Finals in France in 1998. I must have watched it hundreds of times on video but never grow tired of seeing it. It is a good example of what can be done if you have enough confidence in your ability to dribble deep into opposition territory.

When the ball went in the net, what a moment that was. I was mobbed by my teammates and the England fans went wild. But that was nothing compared to the reaction which followed for days and weeks afterwards. It was being compared with the great World Cup goals

skills check

- *Ball control*
- *Balance*
- *Acceleration*
- *Vision*

of all time and I felt immensely proud. Suddenly I was the big news of the day and just about everyone wanted to talk to me.

MY FAVOURITE GOAL

I'll let you into a little secret, here. The World Cup goal against Argentina was the most important but not the best goal I have ever scored. Pride of place in my collection was the one I scored for the England Under-15 side against Scotland at St James' Park back in 1994.

The Scots had just equalised to make it 1-1. At the restart, Kenny Lunt, one of my mates at Lilleshall, passed the ball to me. I was about to knock it back to one of our midfield players when Kenny said: 'Go on. Just run with it!' He had noticed the Scots were still celebrating their equaliser and there was a chance to take them by surprise.

I went past three startled defenders, side-stepping one, and running past a second with a surge of pace. As the third came across to tackle, I feinted to shoot and dragged the ball back as he slid in front of me. Then I curled the ball past the keeper into the top far corner of the net.

It did not create anywhere near the same attention as the Argentina goal, but I do not think I'll ever score a better one than that. It would be near-impossible at professional level because the standard of defending is so high. I've stored it away in my memory bank and occasionally I get the video out to remind me what a special goal it was.

DRIBBLING

43

■ *Running with the ball is an exhilarating feeling and there is no better way to finish than by slotting the ball into the net.*

Beating your opponent

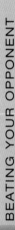

BEATING YOUR OPPONENT

44

As I explained in the section on dribbling, the ability to put a defender out of the game by taking him on and beating him is a fantastic weapon to have. Most of my

'The idea is to throw a defender off balance...'

career I have been able to use my speed and ball control to go past opponents but if you are not blessed with the gift of natural pace, it is worth having a trick or two up your sleeve.

Practice Drill

1 *Move the ball towards the defender, looking at the opponent rather than the ball.*

2 *Crouch low over the ball, transferring your body weight onto your left side.*

3 *Begin a circular motion with the left leg, taking it quickly around the front of the ball, so that the defender follows your movement.*

4 *Transfer your body weight quickly back to your right side while the defender is off balance.*

5 *Before the defender has regained his composure, push the ball away with your right foot and accelerate into space.*

BEATING YOUR OPPONENT

45

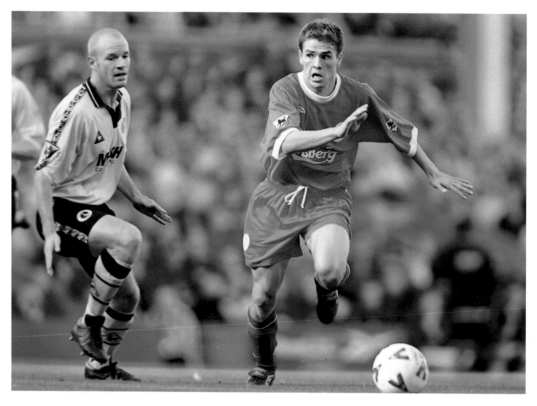

46

ONE AGAINST ONE

The idea is to throw a defender off balance by forcing him to go one way and then sweep past him on the other side. You can dip your shoulder to entice him to lean over and then change direction yourself by moving the ball with the outside of your foot.

A variation on this is the step-over trick. You should swing your foot over the top of the ball and plant it to the side of the ball, leaning your body at an angle as far as you can. Then sweep the ball in the opposite direction with your

Practice Drill

1 *Prepare to carry out the move about 1 metre from your opponent, with the ball close to your leading foot.*

2 *Take the right foot across the ball with the sole of the foot to the outside of your body.*

3 *Without taking your foot off the ball, bring it back across your body with the inside of the same foot.*

Body Feint

Throw the defender off balance with a feint to the left, then sweep past him on the other side.

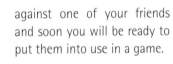

skills check

- *Balance*
- *Body swerve*
- *Speed*
- *Confidence*

other foot while your opponent is still struggling to regain his balance.

PRACTICE BEFORE PLAY

You won't always be able to beat an opponent in a dribble with speed and acceleration. You need to learn to trick a

defender by using your feet, body and ball control to throw him off balance.

Many moves can be used when you are faced by an opponent – but you should practice them at first on your own with a stationary ball. Then use them on the move

against one of your friends and soon you will be ready to put them into use in a game.

47

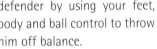
Practice Drill

1 *Kick the ball towards the defender with the trailing right leg and he will move across to block the ball.*

2 *Aim to cannon the ball off your opponent from the outside edge of your front left leading leg.*

3 *The ball will bounce away from the defender into the space to your left, leaving you to continue your run.*

One-on-one with the goalkeeper

A typical Michael Owen goal would be one where I race clear of the defence and find myself one against one with the goal-keeper. Being naturally quick, I have always been able to use my speed to good effect but the hard part comes when you need to beat the keeper. There are a variety of ways of doing this and it can become a real battle of wits.

ELEMENT OF SURPRISE

The keeper will try to stand on his feet for as long as possible without committing himself. If

'Remember, the goalie wants you to make the first move, so try to keep him guessing for as long as possible'

he does this, you have to decide the best moment to shoot and if possible catch him by surprise. A quick, early shot can work before he has had time to set himself in the right position.

As you shoot, keep your eyes on the ball and never look up. It is an old cliché, but the goal never moves and once you are certain of the keeper's position, you can place your

Practice Drill

1 *Once you've made your run and found yourself one-on-one with the keeper, try to commit him into making an early move.*

2 *Fool him into thinking you are going to shoot past him, then drag the ball back across his body.*

3 *You have opened up the goal and should be left with the easy task of rolling the ball into the empty net.*

shot out of his reach. If he has strayed off his line and left you with enough space behind him, you can chip it over his head but you have got to be very accurate and confident to attempt this one. Above all, keep your nerve and once you've made your decision, carry it out with conviction.

SHOOTING ACROSS GOAL
If you are coming towards the goal at an angle, it is usually best to shoot across the keeper towards the far post because if he cannot hold it, there is always a chance a team-mate will be following up to knock in the rebound. But always be prepared to sneak one in at the

■ *This is familiar territory for me, clean through with just the keeper to beat, though it is not always as easy to score as it looks.*

One-on-one with the goalkeeper

The goal can suddenly look very small as the keeper rushes out to meet you, so you have to decide quickly how to deal with the situation. You can choose a chip over the keeper's head or a low drive inside the near post. If you are full of confidence you can sell him a dummy and walk the ball around him.

near post if he has left a big enough gap.

KEEPER COMMITS HIMSELF

If you are bearing down on goal and the keeper makes an early decision to come rushing out and throws himself at your feet, you have to be able to think quickly enough and choose one of several ways to beat him. Remember, the goalie wants you to commit yourself and make the first move so try to keep him guessing as long as possible.

If he has dived in front of you, chip the ball over his body, using the method described in an earlier part of this book, or even scoop it over him by lifting it with the end of your toes. A more difficult option is to side step him and roll the ball into the net. You can feint to shoot and then drag the ball to the side of him with either the inside or outside of the foot. This will open up the goal and leave you with an inviting target.

Whatever way you decide to shoot, it is best to keep a clear head and do not panic, even if you have to make your mind up in a split second.

skills check

- *Composure*
- *Quick-thinking*
- *Accuracy*
- *Ball control*

51

Turning and shooting

I seem to spend half my life on a football field with a defender breathing down my neck. Marking is so tight in the modern game, I almost feel sometimes as if my opponent wants to wear the same shirt as me. But there is no point in complaining. It is a very physical and highly competitive sport and you have to learn to accept the knocks and all kinds of buffeting.

'Marking is so tight in the modern game, I almost feel sometimes as if my opponent wants to wear the same shirt as me'

■ Once you have found the space, you don't have time to waste. Shooting on sight is the best policy.

STAND YOUR GROUND

That does not mean you have to lie down and let a defender walk all over you, though. You must stand your ground and use your body strength to full effect, especially when the tackles are flying in from behind. At Liverpool I work a few days every week in the weights room and do loads of stomach muscle exercises to build the power in my upper body. But I am not in favour of young kids lifting weights and putting too much stress on themselves. A series of sit-ups and press-ups is enough.

The importance of being strong enough to withstand a challenge from behind becomes obvious whenever a ball is played up to a striker with his back to goal. His first thought should be: 'Can I turn my man and get a shot at goal?' The defender will resort to all sorts of tricks to try and stop you.

SHIELDING THE BALL

The first priority is to make sure you keep your body between your marker and the ball. He'll be trying to pull and tug at you to get to the ball, but in some cases you have to give as good as you get without going too much over the top.

Once you have sensed the defender is right at your back

■ *With your marker tight to you, the ability to shield the ball effectively will buy you that extra bit of time and space.*

and the ball is approaching, try to keep him guessing as to what you are going to do. Sometimes you can make a quick lay-off to a team-mate and spin around to look for

the return ball behind the defender.

THROW YOUR MARKER

If you have made your mind up that you are going to turn

Practice Drill

1 *As the ball approaches, keep the defender guessing as to what you intend to do with it.*

2 *Lean against the defender and turn your body against his in a rolling movement.*

3 *Guide the ball the same way as you have rolled with the outside of your foot, using your arms for leverage.*

54

and shoot, make sure you keep your marker in two minds right up to the last moment as to what you are about to do. He won't be able to see the ball in the last few fractions of a second as it arrives at your feet, so that's the time to decide which way to turn.

If he's right up close, lean back either to your left or right and roll your body against him. You should have your eyes glued to the ball and as you are turning drag it to the same side as you are leaning with the outside of your foot until you are in the clear.

Sometimes the defender will make it easier for you by coming at you from the side

so he can get a view of the ball and try to intercept it before it arrives at your feet. If you can hold him off, you will have a clearer chance to turn the ball away from him.

Once you have escaped your marker, you have to make your mind up pretty quickly about your goal attempt. Occasionally you will have the space to take an extra touch and prepare yourself for a shot. But more often than not, you will have to hit the ball first time since the defender will be snapping at your heels trying to get in another tackle.

You might only have had a quick glimpse to see where the goalkeeper is positioned so

sometimes you have to take a guess and go for all-out power to try and beat him. Don't forget the old saying – the goal never moves, so you should always be aware of where the target is and make sure you hit it first time.

Before we leave this section, I must offer a few words of caution about the need not to retaliate. There is nothing more frustrating to a forward than to be clattered from behind by a defender in the sort of situations I have just described. In recent years referees have clamped down on the tackle from behind, but defenders still get away with it from time to time.

4 *With your body between defender and ball, work it into space.*

5 *You only need half a yard, but don't waste it as the defender is close.*

6 *The goal never moves, so always visualise where the target is.*

7 *In a split second you have to decide when to shoot.*

8 *It is often worthwhile just going for shear power at goal.*

9 *Take aim and fire and always be ready to follow up for the rebound.*

TURNING AND SHOOTING

55

skills check

- *Body strength*
- *Close control*
- *Good body roll*
- *Awareness of the target*

MAN-FOR-MAN MARKING

The worst situation I have ever experienced came in an England Under-18 international against Yugoslavia a few years back. In the first 20 minutes, we were awarded ten free-kicks for fouls against me by the same defender. He was simply kicking lumps out of me from behind.

The referee gave us the

free-kicks but took no action against the Yugoslav who was responsible. Eventually I had had enough. When he dumped me on the deck again, I jumped up to complain to the ref and failed to notice that the defender was standing right over me. I caught him full in the stomach with my head. I can honestly say it was a pure accident.

He went down holding his face as though he had been flattened by Lennox Lewis. It was laughable, but the ref came over and showed me the red card. It was the first time I had ever been sent off and, while I was completely innocent, it was very embarrassing, especially as I was captaining my country that night.

The lesson here is a clear one – always keep a cool head. If a defender rattles you and causes you to lose your temper, then he is halfway towards winning the battle with you. It's hard to keep picking yourself up off the ground without complaining, but it's the only way.

■ *This is not a pretty sight for any footballer but is the usual outcome for any player who decides to retaliate.*

57

Volleying

Michael Owen's
SOCCER SKILLS

VOLLEYING

59

Volleying

60

The volley is the most powerful way to kick the ball and strikers need to master the skill because it can produce some tremendous attempts at goal as well as being a crowd pleaser.

TYPES OF VOLLEY

There are two basic ways of volleying, either from a full-on or side-on position. In both instances, timing is vital because you have to meet the ball while it is flying through the air at you. So is balance because you are standing on

'If you can strike your volleys powerfully on target, they are virtually unstoppable'

one leg when you make contact with the ball.

If it is coming at you straight, you have to judge where it is going to land and adjust your position accordingly. You should draw back your kicking foot when the ball has dropped to around hip height. Keep your eyes on the ball and your head down. If you don't, you will not make a clean contact and the ball can fly anywhere.

Volleying from a side-on position is used frequently by forwards because you get so many

Practice Drill

1 *Draw back your kicking leg as the ball drops to around hip height, leaning away from the ball slightly.*

2 *With eyes on the ball and arms outstretched for balance, make contact on the widest part of the boot.*

3 *Follow-through with the kicking leg parallel to the ground and rotate your hips for maximum power.*

VOLLEYING

61

■ *The volley is one of the most dynamic shots in a striker's repertoire.*

crosses flying into the penalty area from the wings. To hit them properly you have to make sure your body shape is right. You have to be certain you are well balanced on your standing leg, draw your striking foot back and rotate your body with a good smooth swing and long follow-through.

VOLLEYING PRACTICE

You should also try to keep your body over the ball to ensure your shot stays low, because it is so easy to balloon it over the bar if you get too far underneath it. Practise at first by getting a friend to throw the ball at you and then have him cross it from a wide position. It might take hours to perfect your technique, but it will be worthwhile.

If you are able to strike your volleys powerfully and on target, the chances are they will be virtually unstoppable.

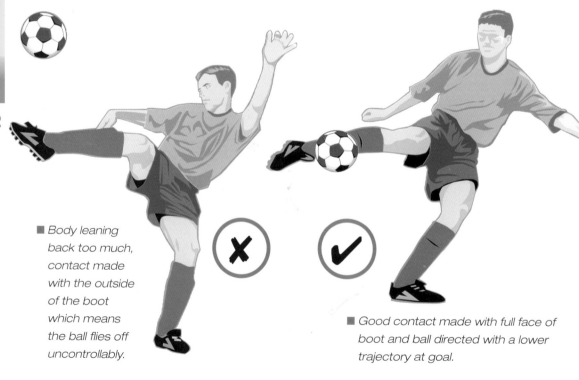

■ *Body leaning back too much, contact made with the outside of the boot which means the ball flies off uncontrollably.*

■ *Good contact made with full face of boot and ball directed with a lower trajectory at goal.*

THE PERFECT VOLLEY

My favourite volleyed goal did not rely so much on power as accuracy. It was scored against Newcastle at Anfield. Jason McAteer crossed the ball in from the right and it came at me much too high to strike first time. But I was able to trap it on my chest and as it dropped I caught it cleanly on the volley. I had already decided to try to lift it over the head of the goalkeeper Shaka Hislop. Now he's a big bloke and it needed plenty of loft to get over his head but I measured it to perfection. It was one of my most pleasing goals because it combined a range of skills, the control of the ball on my chest, the execution of the volley and the judgement of the shot.

skills check

- Good timing
- Balance
- Agility
- Body rotation

Practice Drill

1 *To keep a volley down, make sure you let the ball drop to below hip height.*

2 *Note the low position where contact is made with the ball.*

3 *Rotate the hips and keep your follow-through low.*

VOLLEYING

63

Overhead kick

64

There are few more spectacular sights in football than the overhead kick. Defenders often use them to clear the ball away from the danger zone, and to see a forward launch himself into the air for an attempt at goal is a thrilling piece of action. It is not a skill at which I can pretend to be an expert, and believe me, I know what a difficult exercise it is to perform.

Overhead kicks are also known as bicycle kicks because when you perform them both your feet are off the ground and rotate in a cycling motion as you strike the ball.

If you are a defender, they are an effective way of clearing the ball upfield. If you are a striker, they are an exciting way of shooting at goal and productive too because they can catch keepers by surprise.

'To see a forward launch himself into the air for an attempt at goal is a thrilling piece of action'

■ *Gallic flair and a spectacular overhead kick. David Ginola shows how important it is to keep your eyes firmly fixed on the moving ball.*

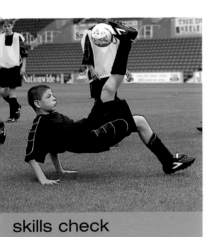

skills check

- *Dexterity*
- *Timing*
- *Good technique*

If they come off, they are admired and applauded. If they don't they can bring howls of laughter, because the player invariably ends up flat on his back and out of the action, with the ball nowhere near where he intended it to be.

KICKING TECHNIQUE

As the ball comes towards you, either from the side or straight on, your kicking foot should be at full stretch, with your

OVERHEAD KICK

■ *The Brazilian Bebeto demonstrates the ideal body position for an effective overhead kick.*

toes reaching for it. You should bend the knee of your non-kicking foot and lean backwards before launching yourself into the air.

Impact with the ball should be made with the flat part of your foot around the bootlace area and your toes should be pointed towards the instep. Your elbows should be bent and your hands spread to break your fall.

PRACTICE APLENTY

If it sounds complicated, that's because it is. It requires hours of practice before it can be perfected and I would not recommend it to beginners because it can lead to a painful fall.

Heading the ball

There are some players – even among the experienced professionals – who do not like heading the ball. The big fear is that it will hurt, but the same rule applies as with chesting the ball down. If you do the exercise properly and use the right part of your body, believe me, it won't hurt.

EYES ON THE BALL
The most common failure among a lot of youngsters is that they close their eyes at the moment they are heading the ball. I suppose that is a natural reaction. If someone hurls something at your face, you tend to flinch and shut your eyes.

If it is a football, you should fix both eyes on the ball and make sure you meet it with your forehead. The following is a useful drill: Bounce the ball in the right place at first and get used to the feel of it. Then throw it higher in the air and try to head it further before teaming up with a pal and start heading it backwards and forwards to each other. Gradually extend the distance until you are about 15-20 yards apart.

'My headed goals are more likely to come at the near post, where I can use my pace to get in front of defenders'

ACHIEVING POWER

When you want to develop more power, the first thing to remember is that it must be achieved by using the upper part of your body.

This means arching your back and thrusting your body forwards as your head moves to meet the ball. A good way to start is from a kneeling position, using a colleague to throw the ball to you and developing that whiplash movement with your body. Then do it from a standing position before eventually throwing the ball in the air and jumping to head it.

HEADING FOR GOAL

A striker needs to be able to head the ball, either when he is laying the ball off as a target man or launching an attempt at goal. The techniques are the same even if the final outcome is different.

Most headers at goal come from crosses out on the flanks and a striker has to be able to time his run properly to meet the ball. If the cross is going to reach the far post or middle of the goal, you have got to be ready to climb above a defender or goalkeeper. That means being brave and trying to avoid the flying heads and keeper's fist. But the basic rules still apply – eyes open, forehead to the ball. If you can develop a good spring in your legs, you can climb above taller opponents.

Practice Drill

1 *Use your arms to get extra leverage as you leap, with eyes focused firmly on the ball.*

2 *Arch the back because this is where you generate some extra power in your header.*

3 *Heading the ball back in the direction from which it has come can often wrong-foot a goalkeeper.*

HEADING THE BALL

67

HEADING THE BALL

Manchester United v Liverpool, FA Cup, 1998

Because of my relative lack of height, I don't score with too many soaring headers in the goalmouth. But there was at least one exception. It came in the game against Manchester United at Old Trafford in the 1998-99 season. Vegard Heggem floated a cross into the six yard box and I managed to climb above Gary Neville and nod it past Peter Schmeichel. It was not until I saw the pictures of it later that I realised how high I had jumped to get to the ball.

68

My headed goals are more likely to come at the near post where I can use my pace to get in front of defenders. The key to this is knowing the players in your own team and looking for the type of cross they are likely to deliver. Sometimes, though, you have to take a gamble and start your run even before the ball has been struck by your team-mate.

It is at times like this that you need an extra pair of eyes. You have to watch the ball in flight right onto your forehead and at the same time keep an eye on your marker to make sure he does not get to the ball ahead of you. You only

Practice Drill

1 *Time your run to the near post so you get there before the keeper.*

Near and far-post headers

• Near post
Time your run to lose your marker to the ball and head down to beat the keeper.

• Far post
Aim for the far corner of the goal, though it is sometimes better to wrong-foot the goalie and head the ball back across goal.

HEADING THE BALL

69

2 *Your feet should be planted firmly to give you a good base for your header.*

3 *Use the pace of the cross to generate power and guide the ball past the keeper.*

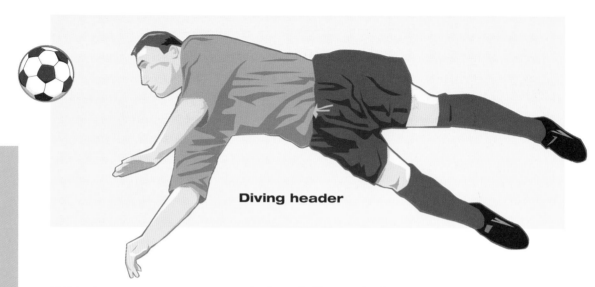

Diving header

■ *If the ball is a fair way ahead, you can still reach it with a diving header. It looks spectacular and can be dangerous because you are throwing yourself into an area where there could be flying boots. But be brave and don't be discouraged.*

need about half a yard of space. If you get there first, you don't need to power the ball but simply use the pace of the cross and direct the ball towards the goal with a late twist of the head.

DEFENSIVE HEADING

I am not called upon much to produce too many defensive headers. Because of my size, that job is best left to taller players in the team. Strikers

tend to be called upon to defend at corners and free-kicks, but my role in these situations is to guard the space just outside the penalty area and stop an opponent getting a free shot at goal if the ball has been cleared. One thing I have been taught when it comes to heading the ball clear is to try to head to a wide position away from the danger area – unless of course you can pick out an unmarked colleague elsewhere.

You have to be careful when defending a high ball not to push your opponent or climb on his back. To give away a free-kick in this sort of danger area can be very costly to your team.

70

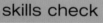

skills check

- *Eyes on ball*
- *Upper body arch*
- *Timing of jump*
- *Anticipation*

Practice Drill

1 *For a defensive header, be aware of where you are on the pitch.*

2 *Get as much height on the ball as possible, full on the forehead, with eyes fixed at all times*

3 *Either head towards a colleague or clear to a wide position away from danger.*

HEADING THE BALL

71

Ball control

The ball is not always going to come at you at a perfect height or weight. Sometimes it will bounce awkwardly in front of you, spinning viciously as it arrives. Other times it will be flying through the air at a strange angle.

But whichever way it arrives you have to be ready to bring it under control, using all parts of the body from your head down to any area of the foot. Only when you have that control can you progress.

'It is important to make a cushioning effect when you receive the ball'

■ *An awkward bounce but you still have to bring the ball instantly under control.*

72

BALL CONTROL DRILLS

The idea is to get the ball under control at your feet as quickly as possible. Often it will mean using the inside or outside of your boot and there are a number of drills which can improve your first touch.

It is important to make a cushioning effect when you receive the ball, whether it is with your foot, thigh, chest, head or even your shoulder. This means being able to draw that particular part of the body away from the ball slightly to soften the impact. It sounds tricky but, as with most skills, you can do it by repeating the exercises over and over again. It is a bit like catching a ball. You don't hold your hands out rigidly otherwise the ball would just bounce straight in and out. You ease them back fractionally to cushion the impact.

■ Try to 'catch' the ball on your instep and drop it at your feet. Draw your controlling foot away slightly at the point of impact.

BALL CONTROL

73

Practice Drill

1 *To control the ball with the inside of your foot, your body should be square on and well-balanced.*

2 *Watch it carefully all the way and allow the ball to drop to around knee height.*

3 *Don't forget to cushion it, withdrawing your foot slightly and allowing the ball to fall at your feet.*

CUSHIONING THE BALL

I can recall a good example of how important it is to be able to control the ball quickly with the outside of the foot. I am never likely to forget it. The goal I scored against Argentina in the 1998 World Cup finals will always be remembered as

Cushioning the ball

*During the lead up to my
memorable goal against
Argentina, my first touch
using the outside of my boot
gave me that crucial yard
of space to surge past
the defender.*

BALL CONTROL

75

a great solo effort but before I
could set off towards the
opponent's goal, I had to control the ball first.

Because of the way it
came at me, I had no time to
collect the ball with the inside
of the foot - which is much

easier. I cushioned it on the
outside of my boot and
brought it into my path so I
could run at the Argentina
defence. This gave me a platform and that crucial extra
yard on the defender to make
my run and score.

Practice Drill

1 *If you are facing the goal and the ball comes at you from the side, you need the outside of your foot to control it.*

2 *Watch the ball all the way onto your foot and use your arms to help with your balance.*

3 *You can allow the ball to drop a little bit lower than if you were using the inside of your foot.*

4 *You still need to deaden the impact as it strikes your foot on the outside area around your toes.*

skills check

- *Good balance*
- *Soften the impact*
- *Use all parts of body*
- *Bend forward*

BALL CONTROL

77

UPPER BODY CONTROL

The higher up the body you go, the more difficult it becomes to control the ball. The thigh is a useful aid, because the ball can be cushioned relatively comfortably and dropped at your feet.

But when you get up to the chest, youngsters often have problems. The important thing to remember is that if you do it properly, it won't hurt. Start by bouncing the ball off your own chest just to get a feel of it. Here's a useful tip. Just as the ball hits you, take a sharp intake of breath because that will draw the chest in and help the cushioning effect.

If you bend forwards as the ball arrives you will be able to guide it down to your feet. Strikers spend a lot of time with their backs to goal waiting to receive the ball, either to hold it up and wait for support or turn to have a go at goal. With a big strong defender at your back, it is important to get that first touch right to prevent him nicking the ball away from you. Whether you are laying it off first time with your feet, thigh, chest or head to a colleague or bringing it down to use yourself, good ball control is VITAL. Only then can you contemplate your next move on goal.

Penalty-taking

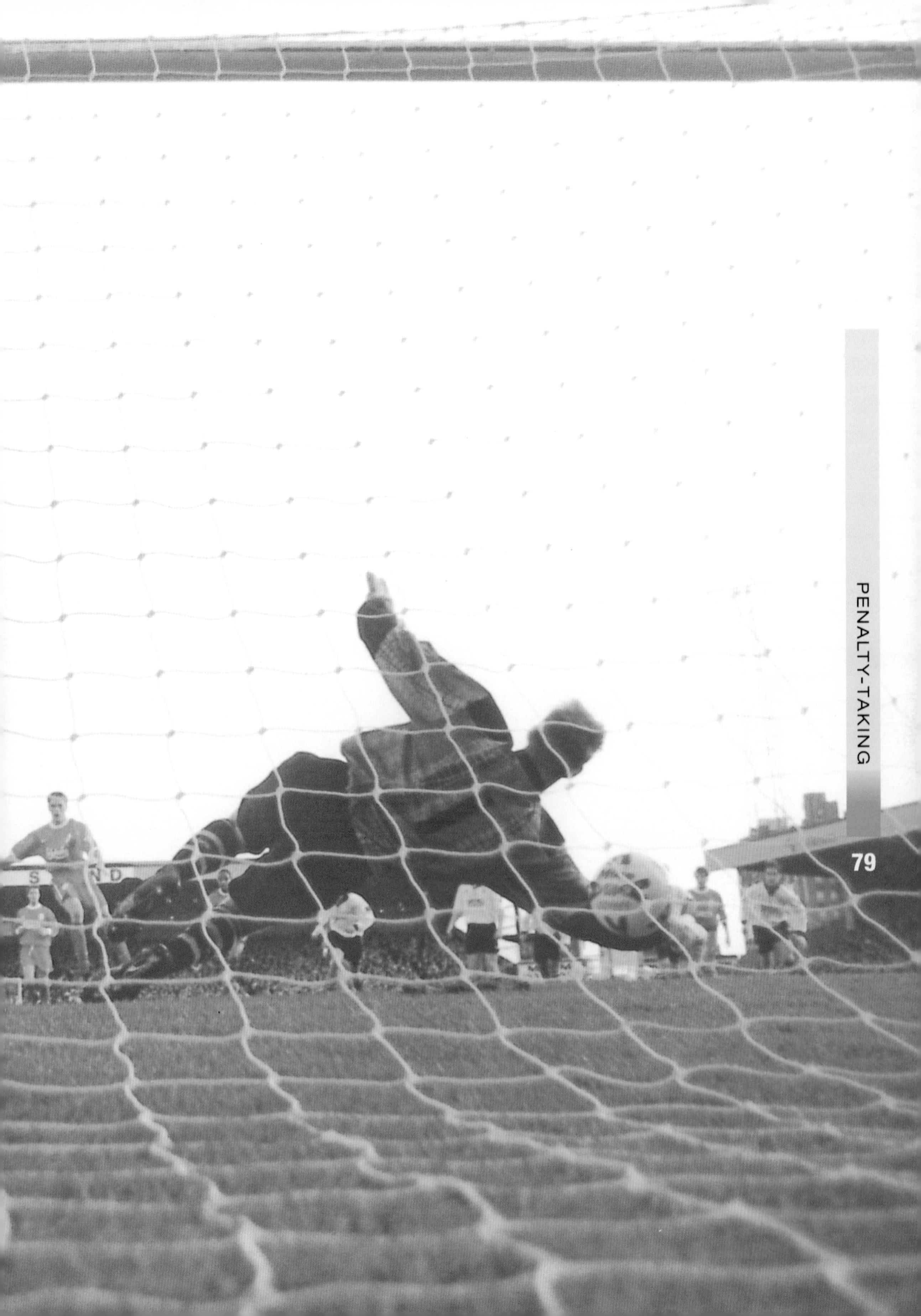

Penalty-taking

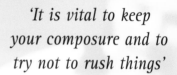

A shot at goal from 12 yards with only the goalkeeper to beat – it sounds like an easy way to score. You should never miss from the spot – or so the pundits tell you – but at the vital moment of a big game with 30,000 or more people watching you, nerves can take over. Suddenly the goal shrinks and the keeper doubles in size. I am not Liverpool's regular penalty-taker, but I usually spend a half-hour each week practising them in training.

KEEP YOUR COMPOSURE

It is vital to keep your composure and to try not to rush things. After placing the ball on the spot, decide the length of your run-up. I usually take six or seven steps and approach the ball at a slight angle.

'It is vital to keep your composure and to try not to rush things'

I never vary this routine because keepers look for a change in your approach and any slight difference will give them a clue about where you are going to shoot. There is so much football on television these days that keepers make a detailed study of all penalty-takers and look for any give-away signs to help them to guess right.

There are two basic methods. You can either wait for the keeper to commit himself to his dive and put the ball into the area of the goal he has left empty. Or you can decide in advance where you are going to place it. I prefer the second way. Once you have made up your mind it is crucial not to change it.

■ *When taking a penalty I prefer placement rather than power.*

Practice Drill

1 *Approach the ball at a slight angle with a run-up of about six or seven paces.*

2 *Aim for the bottom corner but don't look where you are going to place it.*

3 *If you place it accurately and firmly enough, the keeper won't get anywhere near it.*

skills check

- *Good technique*
- *Focus on ball*
- *Accuracy over power*
- *Composure*

Placing your kick

I prefer low and wide, so that the goalkeeper has the furthest to travel to make the save. Dave Seaman is an expert at saving penalty kicks – but, so far, not one of mine!

82

AIM FOR THE CORNER

I always tend to aim for the bottom left or right hand corner of the net, well out of the keeper's reach. On my run-up I keep my eyes fixed on the ball. A glance up to where you are going to put it will easily alert the keeper. I strike it with my instep or side of the foot but don't go for sheer power, just enough to beat the keeper's dive. If it is accurately placed, he won't get near it, even if he has guessed the right way.

I was a regular penalty taker throughout my early career in all the sides I played in from school , through youth football right up to junior international level. But once I joined the senior professional ranks at Liverpool, the management felt that experience was all-important and in my time at Anfield, Robbie Fowler has been first choice. You can imagine my surprise and delight, therefore, when the boss Roy Evans told me before my third game for the first team that I was on penalty-taking duty because Robbie was not playing.

It gave my confidence a real lift to think he had so much faith in me, because I was still only 17. The game was at Wimbledon – where I had scored my first senior goal the previous season – and sure enough, we were awarded a spot-kick when Vinnie Jones brought down Karlheinz Riedle. All the pride and delight I had felt before the game turned to nerves when I stepped up to take it, but I was able to regain my composure and stick to my usual routine. I struck the ball firmly past Neil Sullivan into the bottom right hand corner.

Pressure penalty

When it comes to a pressure situation, nothing could ever compare to the shoot-out after England drew with Argentina in the second stage of the World Cup finals in France. I knew in advance that I would be one of the penalty takers if the match ended all square. Strangely enough, I felt quite relaxed about it as I waited my turn.

I even wandered over towards the area of the ground where I knew my family was sitting. I spotted them and held up four fingers to indicate I was fourth in line. Then I made a stabbing movement on the ground with my foot to suggest to my dad I was going to try to chip the ball over the diving keeper. I could see the look of horror on Dad's face. He knew I never took them like that and it would be a massive risk to change my method. Then he saw me smiling and knew I was only joking.

I also exchanged a few words with Alan Shearer in the centre circle as we waited. I said to him: 'Where do you think I should put it?' His reply was short and to the point: 'Just stick it in the net, like you normally do.' That was a confidence booster from the England captain, who is the best penalty-taker I have ever seen. He combines power with placement and rarely misses.

I stepped forward to take mine with a clear idea of what I was going to do. As I approached the ball, I opened up my body as if I was going to shoot into the bottom right hand corner and then turned at the last minute to put it in the opposite one. The keeper fell for it and dived the wrong way. I lifted my shot more than I usually do and it flew high into the net, just clipping the post. A few inches the other way and it would have bounced back out. It just shows how fine the line is between being a hero and a villain.

PENALTY-TAKING

83

Free-kicks

More and more goals are being scored from direct free-kicks outside the penalty box and most teams have specialists who can bend the ball around a defensive wall from any range up to 35 yards from goal. Jamie Redknapp and Robbie Fowler are our experts at Liverpool, depending on which side of the goal the kick is awarded, and I have to take my place behind them in the pecking order.

The ability to be able to bend the ball around a defensive wall is vital.

■ *Pace can often lead defenders to give away free-kicks.*

'The key to where best to place the ball is the goalkeeper's position'

Practice Drill

1 *Look to see where the keeper is standing before you decide where you are going to put the ball.*

2 *Approach it at a sharp angle and cut across the side of the ball with the instep.*

3 *Lean back slightly to get enough loft on your shot to clear the defensive wall and try to bend it around the outside of the last player or over the top.*

FREE-KICKS

85

Free-kick

It requires great technique to get the ball up and over or around the wall with sufficient pace to beat the keeper, but if you can get it to dip and swerve into either corner, you will have him struggling.

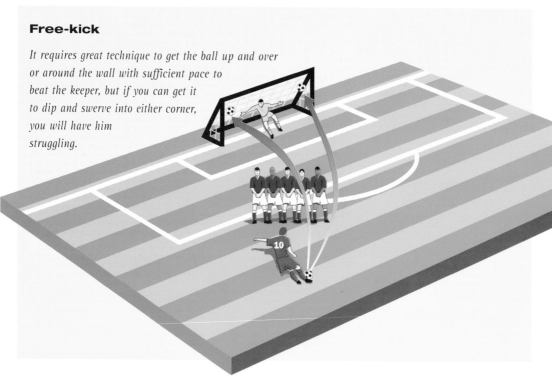

86

DIRECT FREE-KICK

If the direct free-kick is to the left of the goal as you look at it, it is best to use a right-footed player and vice versa. This enables the player to start the flight of the ball towards one area of the goal and swerve it towards another part. The most difficult aspect is to lift the ball over the wall 10 yards away and then get it to dip quickly enough to hit the target.

The key to where best to place the ball is the goal-keeper's position and to which side of the wall he is standing. I always try to go for the biggest gap, though you have to be careful the keeper is not

being clever. Sometimes he will try to fool you by leaving one side of the goal unpro-tected and as you strike your shot, he will dash across his line and swallow it up easily. But a good strong shot with plenty of dip and swerve will cause him problems.

I start my run-up at quite a sharp angle, which gives me enough room to cut across the side of the ball with the inside of my foot which will make it swerve through the air. You also have to get enough loft on your effort to clear the wall, so strike it just under-neath and lean slightly back to lift the ball into the air.

There is also a tendency in

the professional game for players in defensive walls to jump just as you hit your shot to make it even more difficult for you to get the ball over them. Occasionally it might be worth trying to sneak your effort underneath them but if they see it coming, it makes it too easy for them to clear.

INDIRECT FREE-KICK

For this, you obviously need to make a short pass to a team-mate, ie a second player must touch the ball before taking a shot at goal. More often than not, with the wall lined up against the kicker, the player who is receiving the pass has a better view of the goal any-

■ *If you are attacking the penalty area at speed, there is always the likelihood that your marker will give away a free-kick.*

skills check

- *Keeper's position*
- *Clean contact*
- *Good technique*
- *Quick thinking*

way, and maybe even a better angle for the shot. Practice is vital here – what works in training might one day work in a real game situation.

Michael Owen's
SOCCER SKILLS

Corners

Practice Drill

1 *For an outswinging corner, pick out your spot where you intend to land the ball and start your run-up at a slight angle.*

2 *Use the inside of the foot against the outside of the ball to get sufficient swerve to keep the ball away from the keeper.*

3 *Lean back slightly so you can lift the ball into the air and over any defenders who are positioned in the near post area.*

CORNERS

89

Corners

This is not a skill I can pretend to be good at – simply because I never take corners. I would much rather be in the goalmouth, trying to sniff out a scoring chance. But even if you do not take them, it is worth knowing about the different types of corner because it will help you to deal with them – either as a defender or an attacker.

OUTSWINGING CORNER

The basic corner is the outswinger, delivered from the right side of the goal with the right foot or from the left with the left foot. The idea is to curve the ball away from the goalkeeper and his defenders towards the attackers who are making their runs towards goal. The kicker should approach the ball from a slight

■ A perfect near-post corner and the ball is past Peter Schmeichel.

'It is worth working on a few different ones yourself to see if you can catch defences by surprise'

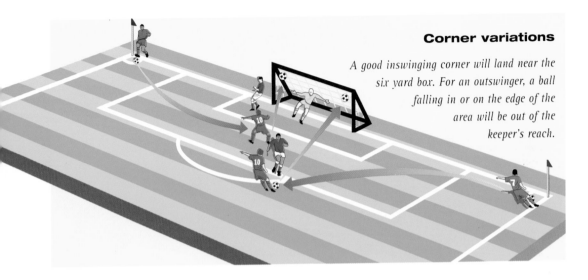

Corner variations

A good inswinging corner will land near the six yard box. For an outswinger, a ball falling in or on the edge of the area will be out of the keeper's reach.

angle and strike it just to the side with the inside of the foot or instep, lofting it into the air by leaning the body back.

INSWINGING CORNER

The in-swinger works in reverse – left foot from the right hand side or right foot from the left. Here you are trying to land the ball deep in the six yard box for you team-mates to attack as they run towards the goal. There are a variety of places to land your corner – either towards the centre of the goal or to the near or far post.

NEAR-POST CORNER

The near post corner has become an extremely popular one because it is so tough to defend against when it is delivered correctly. Position one of your players – ideally one of the tallest members of

the team - just in front of the near post, so he is blocking the keeper's view. Get the corner taker to try and land the ball on his head, either by driving it or floating it towards him.

The person at the near post should then head it backwards across the face of the goal. It only needs the slightest of touches from him to enable team-mates to rush onto it and force it into the net. It is a simple tactic but it causes havoc for defences.

There are all sorts of variations of corners you can work on. Darren Anderton and Teddy Sheringham came up with a good one when they were colleagues for Spurs and England. Teddy would lurk unnoticed just outside the penalty box and just as Darren was about to take the corner he would move forward.

Darren would then pick

him out with his cross and Teddy would volley it, either straight at goal or across the six yard box. It is worth working on a few different ones yourself to see if you can catch defences by surprise.

skills check

- *Balance*
- *Accuracy*
- *Loft on the ball*
- *Lean body back*

Throw-ins

It is amazing how many youngsters are pulled up for foul throws when they first start out. It should not happen because the rules are clearly laid out. You have to keep both feet on the ground, even though there is a tendency to lift one leg off the floor to get more leverage. The ball has to go back over your head before you bring it forward and release it. The temptation is to just drop in from near the top of your head if a colleague is close to you.

SHORT THROW

Most teams have experts for long throw-ins, but every player has to be ready to pick the ball up and take a quick throw if necessary and catch a defence on the hop.

You can either throw it to an unmarked colleague who is racing towards your opponents' goal, or you can look for a quick return pass if your team-mate is closely marked. Throw it to him at a comfortable height and speed so he can reach it before his marker gets to the ball. You can aim at any part of his body: foot, thigh, chest or head.

Your team-mate will try to hold his defender off and play the ball back to your feet. You should be on your toes and ready to receive the ball back from him. Even before

Practice Drill

1 *Bend your knees and arch your back.*

2 *Release the ball just as it passes in front of your head.*

■ *Note how the ball is taken right back between the shoulder blades.*

THROW-INS

93

Practice Drill

1 *Hold the ball firmly in your hands, arms outstretched in front of you, and point it towards the target area.*

2 *Take about half-a-dozen steps towards the touchline and begin to bring the ball back over your head.*

3 *Do not step over the line and be sure the ball almost touches a point between your shoulders.*

'The long throw has become an attacking weapon for lots of teams'

THROW-INS

94

you have got it, you should be looking for your next move, either to run with it or play a pass to another colleague.

LONG THROW

The long throw has become an attacking weapon for lots of teams and in the right hands it is as good as a corner. It is best to have a good run-up if you

are trying to hurl the ball into the danger area. Half a dozen steps should be enough. As you approach the touchline – be careful not to step over it – plant one foot forward and arch your back with the ball held firmly in both hands.

Do not strain too hard as you transfer the weight of your body forwards – a bit like

a javelin thrower would – and you can then deliver a looping throw or one with a much flatter trajectory.

It is worth practising these in training with one of the good headers of the ball in your team. Try to land the ball onto his head from a range of distances, starting from 20 metres and building up.

4 Begin to swing your arms through with a nice flowing movement, your back slightly arched.

5 Release the ball just in front of your head, aiming for height as well as distance.

6 Follow through with the arms and be ready to move off and look for a return pass.

THROW-INS

95

■ See how the fingers and the thumbs are placed behind the ball to help you throw it in the right direction.

skills check

- Feet on ground
- Arched back
- Bent knees
- Follow through with hands

Defending

One of the most important lessons to learn in football is that defending is not just for defenders. I was taught from a very early age that defending starts from the front. In other words, it is up to strikers to put their opponents under pressure as soon as they have the ball and stop them building their moves from the back.

■ *Getting ready to stop Manchester United's Gary Neville surging forward with the ball.*

Practice Drill

1 *Deny the defender space by keeping as close to him and the ball as possible.*

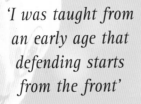

'I was taught from an early age that defending starts from the front'

DEFEND FROM THE FRONT

I have had to improve this part of my game since turning professional. My job as a striker is not to go diving into tackles all the time. I have to close down opponents, jockey them and force them into hurried clearances. I also have to deny them the space to pass the ball where they can find an unmarked team-mate.

That means taking up a position to the side of the defender and blocking off the route where he wants to pass the ball. I have to open out my body and force him to put it into an area where he does not want to go.

2 *Block off one area and force him to take the ball where he does not want to go.*

Defending space

OWEN

As a striker you have got to be prepared to run and harass defenders into making hurried clearances. It requires a lot of energy and persistence to chase the ball backwards and forwards between defenders in 20-30 metre sprints, but is well worthwhile if it means winning the ball back for your team. At Liverpool down the years, players like Ian Rush and Peter Beardsley were experts at doing this.

DEFENDING

98

Often strikers have to operate in a situation where two of them are up against four opponents, so that requires a lot of chasing and pressurising them into making hasty decisions. It is a very unglamorous part of a striker's job and you rarely have a lot to show for it – except the thanks of your team-mates if you do it well. Don't forget, football is a team game and it is not always about the glory of scoring goals.

DEFENDING AT FREE-KICKS AND CORNERS

I rarely find myself back in my own half having to defend opposition attacks. That is best left to those players who are experts at this sort of thing. But I do have a role to play at set-pieces.

At free-kicks and corners, I take up a position just outside the penalty area. I am not given a marking job. It is my duty to guard the space outside the box. Then, if the ball is cleared out to an opponent, I have to make sure he doesn't get a clear strike at goal.

Of course, if I carry out my defending successfully and gain possession of the ball, it means that a swift counter-attack is possible from deep. Turning defence into attack is one of the most potent weapons in a team's armoury, especially if you have players with pace and the ability to spot a colleague in space further up the field.

■ *You have to be tough and aggressive sometimes to get the better of a defender when he has possession of the ball.*

TURNING DEFENCE INTO ATTACK

Even from a defensive position I am looking for an opportunity to score. The opposing team will usually leave two defenders to mark one of our players when they are attacking our goal at a set-piece and send the rest of their players forward. I will try to spot an opening to counter-attack them. I can use my pace to latch onto a clearance and catch them on the break while they still have players in our half of the field.

DEFENDING

99

skills check

- *Jockey opponent*
- *Close down space*
- *Vision*
- *Anticipation*

Tackling

'A striker
has to play
his part in
breaking up
the other
team's attacks'

■ *A well-executed sliding
tackle can bring you
to an abrupt halt.*

It is not what I'm best at, but sometimes I have no alternative but to tackle an opponent. As I have explained previously, a striker has to play his part in breaking up the other team's attacks and if it means having to get stuck in, I am quite happy to do so. You must be able to tackle cleanly.

Michael Owen's

BLOCK TACKLE

The block tackle is the most commonly used and the most effective because you are using the widest area of your foot on the inside of your boot. It can also be the most risky because if you do not put your full weight into the challenge, it can cause injuries to the ankle or knee joints.

You have to be able to withstand the full force of your opponent, who will be running at you with the ball or trying to clear it. You should put your non-tackling foot alongside the ball and meet it with the inside of your other foot, leaning forwards slightly and putting all your body weight into the challenge at the point of impact. Don't pull out of it once you have committed yourself or you will risk getting injured.

STAB TACKLE

The stab tackle can be used when you are not in a position to get your body into the challenge. As you approach your opponent from the side, nip in ahead of him and stab the ball away from him with your out-stretched foot. It tends to be used by a full back to prod the ball into touch as a winger is trying to beat him on the outside. But it can also become a way of starting your own attacking moves. If you see a team-mate in an unmarked position as you are making your tackle, stab the ball towards him and look for the return while your opponent is out of position.

TACKLING

101

Make sure your full weight goes into the **block tackle** to avoid the risk of injury.

For a **stab tackle**, which usually takes place side-on to your opponent, reach out for the ball and stab it away with the end of your foot to stop him in full flight.

SLIDING TACKLE

The sliding tackle should only be used as a last resort. You should always stay on your feet if you can, but if your opponent is too far away for you to use the block or stab, you can slide your body underneath him and force the ball away. Again, timing is all-important. Keep your eyes on the ball and your body as low as possible and try to make a clean contact.

If your timing is good and you are really clever, you can force the ball off your opponent's legs and win your team a throw-in.

HOOK TACKLE

An interesting variation on the sliding tackle is the hook. The technique is the same, but instead of losing possession you scoop the ball away from your opponent. As you win it, you get to your feet as quickly as possible with the ball under control and you are off on the counter-attack. Manchester United's Ryan Giggs uses this ploy very effectively.

Speed is vital, both in winning the ball and getting away.

LATE TACKLES

Tackling is be a hazardous business – and not just because it can cause injuries. Anything fractionally late can send an opponent tumbling to

For the **sliding tackle**, keep your body as low as possible and try to make a clean contact as you slide underneath your opponent and accelerate away.

For the **hook tackle**, your foot hooks around the ball to force it out of your opponent's possession, and then you're ready to jump to your feet and accelerate away.

the ground and with it comes the threat of the referee reaching for a yellow or red card. I have had my fair share of yellow cards, but I can honestly say I have never deliberately gone out to foul an opponent. It has usually been for mistimed or over-enthusiastic challenges.

TACKLING

102

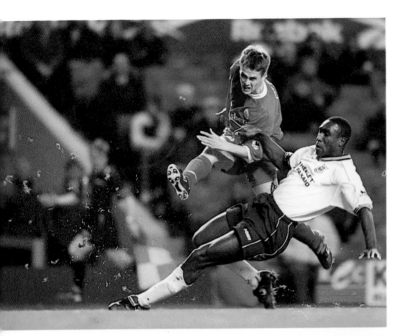

skills check

- *Timing*
- *Speed*
- *Agility*
- *Strength*

TACKLING

103

Red mist in Manchester

I have only received two red cards in my career. I have already explained my sending-off when I was captain of the England Under-18 side against Yugoslavia for which I was completely innocent.

The second time was against Manchester United in season 1997–98. I was booked first for a high challenge on Peter Schmeichel. I went in for a ball with my foot up. It was reckless but not malicious and he made a bit of a meal of it by throwing himself through the air. Even so, I could not complain about the booking.

Later in the game as Ronny Johnsen tried to clear the ball, I went sliding in and was a fraction late getting there. I caught him with my foot and the referee showed me a second yellow card and then a red. It was pointless complaining. Cards are handed out with increasingly regularity nowadays and you have to accept them as an occupational hazard.

Goalkeeping

GOALKEEPING

104

Let me make one thing clear. I don't like goal-keepers. I have nothing personal against them, but it is just that I have spent my whole life trying to get the better of them. They are the enemy as far as I am concerned. I have never played in goal – not even as a youngster – and have no desire to stand between the posts and use myself for target practice.

'Agility, bravery plus a good safe pair of hands... essential requirements for a goalie'

QUALITIES OF A GOOD KEEPER

That does not mean I do not admire keepers for their agility and bravery. Those two qualities plus a good safe pair of hands are the essential requirements for a goalie and they also need sound judgement about when and when not to come off their line.

They have their own specialist training routines and exercises. They say you have to be a bit crazy to be a keeper and I would not argue with that. They seem to spend hours on the training pitch, throwing themselves around on hard grounds and working out various angles.

Since the introduction of the back pass rule, kicking has also become an essential part of a goalkeeper's trade and they have to spend time in training, booting the ball clear while under pressure from outfield players.

1 *You have to be agile to get across your goalmouth.*

2 *Try and get a good strong hand to the ball to force it around the post or away from the danger area.*

3 *Sometimes you can only touch it away with your fingertips.*

Practice Drill

1 *An awkward dipping shot can often catch a keeper off his line.*

2 *Adjust your position and stretch high into the air.*

3 *Give the ball a strong flick with your wrist to force it over the crossbar.*

FIRST LINE OF ATTACK

A good goalkeeper will also be able to play his part as an attacker. Once he has the ball in his hands he should always be looking for a quick throw or clearance to a team-mate.

The really outstanding keepers will be able to sling the ball almost half the length of the field to set a forward on the move. It is well worth spending 15 minutes in each training session developing the strength of your throws.

An accurate kicked clearance is also a worthwhile way to catch opposition defences on the wrong foot. Practice volleying and half-volleying the ball out of your hands for both distance and accuracy.

Spring into the air to catch a cross and always try to reach it at its highest point.

skills check

- *Agility*
- *Sound judgment*
- *Bravery*
- *Good kicking ability*

GOALKEEPING

106

1 *A safe pair of hands are a vital requirement for all goalkeepers.*

2 *Eyes on the ball and wrap your fingers around it.*

3 *Hold on tight because there may be a forward looking for the rebound.*

GOALKEEPING

107

Tricks of the trade

We all love to watch those players who have a special trick that they can put into the game. They are magical moments which have fans up off their seats. I remember watching Paul Gascoigne producing some amazing tricks in the 1990 World Cup finals in Italy. Let's have a look at a few of them.

BACK-HEEL

The back heel is an unexpected pass which is used to direct the ball in the opposite direction to which we are facing. It can catch the defender completely by surprise – but the problem is your team-mate might not be expecting it either! So make sure you indicate or call to your team-mate as you make the pass. Strike the ball firmly with your heel and only use it over short distances.

NUTMEG

A nutmeg is a very basic way of beating an opponent. Shape as though you are going to pass or shoot the ball to either side of your opponent. As he stretches to intercept and opens his legs, quickly slot the ball through the gap and carry on to collect it the other side.

MORE TRICKS

All of the following moves can be used to trick an opponent in order to beat him:
• Hit the ball with the inside of one foot against the inside of the other so that it rebounds in the other direction and takes you away from the confused defender.
• When receiving the ball, step over it with your left foot, taking the defender to your left and accelerate away to the right.

'I remember watching Paul Gascoigne producing some amazing tricks in the 1990 World Cup finals in Italy'

108

Practice Drill

1 *Shape as though you are going to sweep past the defender.*

2 *The defender faces with the legs slightly apart. Sidefoot the ball through the gap.*

3 *Try to play the ball at a slight angle so that you can run on to it and accelerate away.*

TRICKS OF THE TRADE

109

Practice Drill

1 Approach to a distance of about 1 metre from your opponent.

2 Roll the sole of the right foot across the ball, towards your left side.

3 As it comes across you, step over it in the other direction with your left foot.

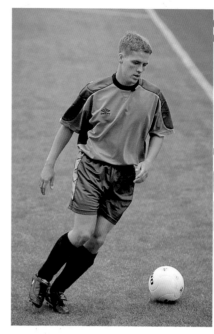

5 Step back out and push the ball off with the outside of your left foot.

6 You are out in the clear, having pulled the defender in the opposite direction.

7 Accelerate away from your opponent, being careful to maintain your balance.

4 *The defender will be confused, having initially followed the rolling ball.*

8 *This trick is known as 'The Ronaldo' and is a handy skill to have.*

• Stop the ball between both feet, grip it tightly and jump past an opponent.

• Again grip it tightly between both feet, but this time lift the ball behind you before turning your feet towards your opponent and tossing it over his head so you can run onto it.

• Step over the ball to the inside with your right foot as though you are going to pass. Miss the ball and the defender will follow. Bring the ball away with the outside of the same foot and accelerate away beyond the defender.

JUGGLING WITH THE BALL

Whoever said juggling was only for the circus was wrong. Not only is it fun to do, it can help a player improve all aspects of his game – notably his touch and confidence on the ball.

Start by bouncing the ball on your foot and see how many times you can keep it in the air. As you improve, flick it up onto your thigh, then your head and even your shoulder. When you have got a good feel for the ball, try and catch it on the back of your neck.

You don't have to do this drill on your own. Juggle it back and forwards with a pal or even among a group of you and if you want to be really flash use more than one ball between you.

Although continuous juggling may not be used too often in a game, it is the best way to develop and improve your first touch. You can get great control of the ball using a variety of body parts. Try to use your feet, thighs, ankles, heels, head, shoulders – anything other than your arms and hands.

Try these juggling tricks:

• Juggle using the outside of one foot. You will need to lock your foot in a position horizontal to the ground and allow the ball to bounce off the centre part of the outside foot.

• Allow the ball to bounce in a juggle, and step over to the

■ *Juggling with the ball using the outside of the right foot.*

■ *Other tricks: flicking the ball up with the heel of the trailing leg (left) and balancing it on the back of the neck (right).*

middle, missing the ball and then flick it back up with the heel of the trailing leg.

• While juggling the ball on one foot, come 360 degrees (a full circle) around the ball and resume juggling without it touching the floor.

GETTING THE BALL INTO THE AIR

• Pinch the ball between the back inside of both feet. Leap in the air with the ball, turn and catch the ball on your foot.

• With the ball in front of you, quickly bring

112

TRICKS OF THE TRADE

both feet together and under the ball and watch the spin lift it into the air.

• With a partner feeding you a rolling ball, step over it with one foot and flick it into the air with the trailing leg.

• Try to catch the ball when juggling on the area of the boot near your laces. Cushion it as it drops and try to hold it for five seconds. Then try to catch it between the thigh and stomach.

• Balancing the ball on the forehead, nose or behind the neck is more difficult but perfectly possible with practice.

■ Keeping the ball in the air while stretched out on the ground is a good form of exercise.

skills check

• Constant practice
• Sure-footedness
• Agility
• Balance

TRICKS OF THE TRADE

113

Skills games

115

Skills games

FUTEBOL DE SALAO

There are lots of opportunities now to play small-sided games on shortened pitches with a smaller ball and goalposts. They are great fun and give you the chance to put your skill on the ball into use. One game I learned about recently

> *'I developed my early skills in two-against-two matches with my dad and brothers in the park'*

was imported into this country from Brazil by Simon Clifford, a football coach based in Leeds.

It is called *Futebol de Salão* – which means 'Football of the Dance Hall'. Apparently it became popular in Brazil in the 1920s and 1930s when they ran out of space to play football outside in the parks. So they took it indoors into the dance halls. In order to avoid causing too much damage, they did not use a full-size ball. They used a smaller one and filled it with foam and air.

These components of the ball mean that it is very hard. It is difficult to kick long distances and that encourages short, sharp, passing and individual skills. There is no place in this kind of game for the big brawny types who can belt the ball the full length of the field.

116

Y[ou] can practise all the skills you want but eventually you have to put them all together in a game. That is when you discover whether all the hard work is worthwhile. It does not have to be a full-blown organised match. I developed my early skills in two-against-two matches with my dad and brothers in the park.

15–17m

25–30m

6m

■ *Pitch for futebol de salão.*

■ *Futebol de salão is fast and exciting.*

As it grew in popularity, it became the game all the youngsters took part in, and such great players as Pele, Ronaldo and Juninho all started out in *futebol de salão*. More and more English clubs are using it now to develop their youngsters' skills and it is easy to see why.

SMALL-SIDED MATCHES

There are other versions of mini-soccer, using a bigger, conventional ball on a larger pitch. This enables you to spread the game out a bit and involves longer passing, shooting and volleying.

Professional teams use these types of game and over the years they have become a significant part of training at club and international level. Liverpool Football Club is famous for its five-a-side matches and we rarely finish a day's

■ *The size-2 ball used in futebol de salão is much smaller than a conventional size-4 football.*

SKILLS GAMES

■ *Simon Clifford, coaching consultant on this book and the man who introduced futebol de salão to this country from Brazil, takes a break to chat with me and the children.*

118 work without a highly competitive game. You can introduce all sorts of restrictions to make them more interesting like one-touch, two-touch, only using your weaker foot, the ball has to be touched by every member of the team before you can score or you can only score with a header. Sometimes we even play eleven-a-side using a smaller area of the pitch. This really gets you thinking and your feet moving quicker.

These games can provide loads of enjoyment but, more than that, they create the types of situations you are going to meet in a real match. Have fun with them – but treat them seriously. Next time it could be the real thing.

FOR MORE INFORMATION

For those of you wanting to find out more about futebol de salão, you should contact the following:

UK Confederation of Futebol de Salão
34 Chandos Place
Leeds
West Yorkshire
LS8 1QS
Tel: 0113 269 4143
www.futebol-de-salão.co.uk

Recovering from injury

There is nothing more frustrating in a footballer's life than to be laid off with an injury. To have to spend hour after hour in the treatment room while your team-mates are training and playing matches is a horrible experience, though we have to accept that no professional can go through an entire career without suffering some sort of physical setback.

MY INJURY AT ELLAND ROAD

I have been fortunate in my career so far – touch wood – to escape anything too serious but I know what it feels like to be ruled out of action for a prolonged period after suffering a torn hamstring at the end of the 1998-99 season. It had been giving me problems for a few weeks and eventually went during a match against Leeds United. I knew from talking to my colleagues it was the sort of injury which takes several months to repair, and caution and patience would be needed before I could get back to playing again.

The fact that I tore my muscle had nothing to do with me failing to go through my warm-up preparations properly that night. As a striker who relies on speed off the mark and sudden explosive bursts of acceleration, a great deal of strain and pressure is put on my hamstrings.

So when my right hamstring went, it was simply a question of wear and tear. I was glad, in a way, that the injury happened so close to the end of the season, which meant I could spend all of the summer recuperating and having treatment and did not miss as many Premiership games as I would have done if it had happened in mid-season.

'As with all injuries, you should listen to medical opinion'

TAKE MEDICAL ADVICE

As with all injuries, the first lesson I had to learn was to listen to medical opinion and obey all the instructions and advice given to me by the Liverpool staff. With so much money invested in players nowadays, no club can afford to cut corners when it comes to treatment of injuries and at Anfield we enjoy the best facilities available.

Medical science has moved forward so much that expensive equipment is widely used, both in the detection and treatment of injuries. I found myself having regular scans, laser and massage treatment just to repair the tear. Then it was a question of building the strength back into the muscle.

It was a slow and painstaking process but throughout it all I was lucky to be in the hands of Liverpool FC's experts in this field. At one point, after suffering some slight discomfort

■ *A hamstring injury can be caused by wear and tear.*

while working out on an exercise machine while we were in pre-season training in Switzerland, I was sent to a German clinic to see a top specialist who gave me my own programme to make sure my muscles were strengthened and developed in a balance way.

Now I know youngsters cannot expect to receive the same specialised care and attention as those of us in the professional game, but the essential rules are still the same. Get the best advice available and always listen to it. There is always the temptation to rush back into action too quickly, but that is a foolish option. An extra week to recover is always better than coming back too soon and breaking down again, because

injury recovery plan

- *Get the best medical advice available.*
- *Take a complete rest from the game.*
- *Do not be tempted to rush your recovery.*
- *Slowly build the strength back into the affected area.*

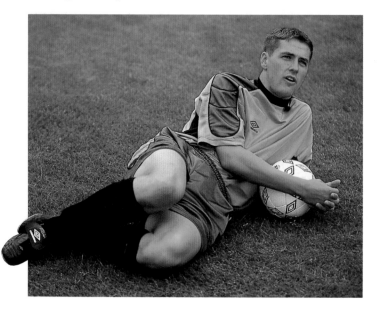

that is guaranteed to force you back onto the treatment couch for another long spell.

There will sometimes be pressure from managers and coaches to force you into a speedy recovery, but you must resist this and take your lead from the medical people.

I know you will be itching to get back into the real action but patience has to be the keyword.

■ *It is not always easy to lie around doing nothing!*